£3.25

Written by John Kercher

All text copyright © Grandreams Limited, 1985.
All photographs copyright © Richard Francis.

The Publishers wish to thank TI Raleigh Limited for their help
in producing this annual.

Published by

GRANDREAMS LIMITED
Jadwin House, 205/211, Kentish Town Road, London, NW5 2JU.

Printed in Holland

ISBN 0 86227 319 6

# CONTENTS

# ANDY RUFFELL

## ~ "what BMX has done for me."

# ANDY RUFFELL
## ~"what BMX has done for me."

What Barry Sheene did for motorbike racing, Andy Ruffell has done for the sport of BMX. Not just for his expert handling of the bike, but his engaging personality and devotion to competition riding.

Since he began riding in the early 1980s, he has developed into not just a racer, but also a television presenter at most of the major meets, and is also a businessman. He regards himself as a free-lance agent to some extent, although he is now signed to the Raleigh team, with whom he has now been racing for a year.

He says that his own introduction to the sport came as a natural progression from normal cycling, and it was only discovering a race meet that he became involved in

# ANDY RUFFELL
## ~"what BMX has done for me."

competition racing. "I went in for that event in late 1980 and won," he says."It made me feel really good and I thought then that this was a sport that I wanted to take further."

That he did, by becoming British Champion on three separate occasions as well as British Freestyle Champion once. "But then I only entered once," he laughs. "Now I tend to concentrate much more on racing than the Freestyle competitions, although I still do exhibitions of the various skills."

He admits that his approach to training for racing is much more demanding than for freestyle.

"It's not just a case of practising with the bike," he says. "I probably spend something like six hours every day in some form of physical exercise to build up my strength. This might take the form of running, work outs at a gymnasium and riding. I'm always trying to keep up my standards and improve on them.

"As for Freestyle, well, like I said, I don't compete on that level now, just put on shows."

The freestyle competitions are, he says, changing in the way they are conducted now. There used to be a couple of distinct categories. Normal riders fell into three classes according to age and in competition there would be certain compulsory movements that had to be effected by each rider. These would comprise of, say a roll back, front wheel hop, a switcharound, kick turn, an aerial, back hop and frame stand. This would be followed by one minute of improvisational freestyle and

# ANDY RUFFELL
## ~"what BMX has done for me."

points would be awarded to each individual.

The Master or Expert Class would not be geared to compulsory movements, but to total improvisation for 1 ½ minute duration where points would be awarded on the basis of continuity, style, ease of movement, originality and performance.

"Now," says Andy, "you find that there aren't so many compulsory movements, it is all done on improvisation."

Andy, of course, has now moved up from normal competition racing to the professional circuit and that is now enabling him to become involved in more activities outside of the physical side of the sport.

"I have my own promotions company and a leisure wear set up too," he says. "Then I'm also involved in doing quite a lot of television presentation of events as well as appearances and so forth. It really is a full time job now."

This must, however,

present problems for him as a racer, "Oh, it does," he laughs. "Like last time when I did the Kellogg's Championships. I was doing commentary for the cameras as well as riding and it wasn't too easy jumping backwards and forwards between the two. Now I've managed to get a bit better at handling it."

He is also proud of the fact that his early morning weekend show on BMX riding drew a greater audience than Saturday Superstore. "That was particularly pleasing," he says.

Andy also receives quite a sack of letters each month, all of which he answers, and are usually related to how to perform certain tricks on bikes, or how riders can improve their starts at competitions.

Andy says that the professional circuit in Britain is increasing. "At present there are something like a couple of dozen of us, and I enjoy it a great deal. The prize money is pretty good too, as there is around

# ANDY RUFFELL

## ~"what BMX has done for me."

£40,000 on offer. In the Kellogg's Championships there is almost £2,500 per race, which isn't bad.

"I'll probably stay professional for quite a number of years, because I'm already racing against some American professionals who are well into their mid-twenties. But then in America, they've had the professional circuit for around 15 years and they're much more established there!"

Andy has already been to America three times to compete, not to mention most of Europe. "The next countries I'm racing in are probably going to be Japan, Canada and Australia," he says enthusiastically. "I'm really looking forward to that because I haven't been there before and it'll be a new experience."

He admits that on some occasions he has come up against poor tracks on his travels. "But mostly they are in good shape," he says. "I think we have some good

ones in Britain. It's all been a matter of educating people as to what is required for good competitions. I don't think that there are many improvements that can be made. I certainly don't have any complaints."

When the BMX sport began to take off here there were some apprehensions about whether it could function properly when there were two organizations running it.

"There might have been some hassles originally with the UKBMX and the NBMXA," says Andy. "But any of the problems have been ironed out now. The associations are getting stronger if anything and I think that they realised that they had to work closely together.

"We now have a Professional Riders' Association too, and we have to work closely with both the UKBMX and the NBMXA, and so there isn't any rivalry. Everything is done for the good of the sport."

# ANDY RUFFELL
## ~ "what BMX has done for me."

He does think that the quality of the racing might improve, however and says: "Riders are getting much faster now and I think this is because a lot of them are realising that if they want to improve, it's not just a case of turning up at meetings and racing. They've learnt that they must put in the hours of practising during the week.

"I think that in the future we might see more girls and fellas competing against each other. It's a misconception that there are separate races for each. There is no strict ruling to this. If a girl wants to compete in a boys race she can, and there are a few that do."

As for Andy, he sees his future in television. "But not for several years yet. I've a lot more winning to do on the world's tracks."

# SAFETY
## –CLOTHING FOR CAREFUL RIDERS

Whilst a lot of people might regard BMX riding as a fun sport, this is no reason to ignore safety factors. Like any activity, there should be careful attention paid to make certain that no one is going to get hurt. And that doesn't just mean the riders, but the spectators too. Irresponsible riding by any individual is something to be discouraged.

For not only can this cause injury possibly to someone who has just come to watch, it can also make things tough for other riders. Rules for racing must be strictly adhered to, then.

Perhaps what has changed most in recent times has been the toughening up of various 'safety' accessories which riders wear. Crash helmets have always been a must for anyone racing in competition. But they used to be made to sustain just a good knock. This has changed in that the kind of speeds some riders are achieving in competition can be anything around the 40 m.p.h. level.

It is only common sense to make absolutely certain, then, that the type of crash helmet worn is a safety

approved one. At those speeds you need something tougher than those helmets that can just take a good knock. There are plenty around which are of sufficient lightweight content for BMX riding whilst retaining the necessary strength to sustain a tumble.

Accessories for body safety have also come more into their own. There was a time when many of the safety gear worn was for 'show' rather than protection. This might have been okay originally but now the gear must do the proper job. Fingerless gloves are a welcome product for most riders as normal gloves were considered to hamper the fine touch steering which most riders enjoy. Now they can avoid scuffed knuckles and still use that fine touch.

Protective padding to the elbows is also advisable, as it is to the knees and shins. These paddings can either be bought individually to suit or be incorporated into special race jeans.

A face mask is also a good buy since it is not just the possibility of falling off that makes it advisable, but also stray pieces of dirt and grit that might be thrown up during intensely competitive racing.

Of paramount importance, of course, is the bike itself. There should never ever be anything sticking out from the machine which could possible injure another rider. And all joints, brakes and other stress points should be regularly inspected for the rider's own safety.

Most of these things are basic common sense, but then the obvious, being so, is often neglected!

# SAM WOOD

~ "my role as the
Raleigh Team Manager."

*P*erhaps what has become one of the most important jobs in BMX team riding is that of team Manager. When the sport was in its infancy, many of the riders were left to their own devices, only coming together for the important competition events. But now the Manager is as decisive a factor in winning points for the team as the rider and the quality of the bike used.

Sam Wood is Manager of the Raleigh team and highlights here the varied duties that he has to perform to ensure that his boys obtain the maximum for their efforts. Yet, surprisingly, he was only drawn into management as a result of buying his own son a BMX machine.

"I confess that at first I thought it was just another bike with flashy trimmings," he says. "But after my son won a couple of events I began to take much more interest in the sport. This led to me looking after his bike at competitions and then the invitation to do some commentating. Slowly I found more of my time was being involved in the BMX circuit until eventually I was asked by Raleigh to manage their team."

Now his work in that capacity takes him around the world to the various competitions, marshalling his team like a crack unit.

"The important aspect of my job," he says, "is in the area of track operations. At its most basic, the vital ingredient is in presentation. I make absolutely certain that the team van looks good, with plenty of stickers and banners to announce just who we are and that we mean business. Also that the boys are turned out well too. I want them to look like the winners they are before they even mount the saddle!"

The next stage in his preparation at a race meeting is attention to the bikes. "It's not been unknown for me to strip all of the bikes down at least four times to try and improve their efficiency, from the moment that we arrive to their moving to the starting gate," he says. "Even when you are positive everything is alright it doesn't do any harm to check for fine cracks in the frame even though this is rare. I'll also strip out the bearings and tighten the spokes. That can make all the difference between coming in a winner or second!"

What Sam also tries to avoid, is too much pressure being applied to his riders by the usual administrative work at meets. "So I attend to the registration of the boys, make certain that their race numbers are all in order, and then get them all sat down behind a table and tell them to relax."

He is also pleased with the fact that he can field a complete bike from spares if he has to. "I try to keep every necessary part available on the van," he says, "and regularly work with a check list to replace those things we use up at meetings. Organization is the keyword."

He says that with nine riders aged between 10 and 18 years old, they all need some kind of attention. "Making certain that they run up, that their helmet hasn't snapped or that they haven't forgotten anything. All of this is so important because a rider must be completely concentrating on the race itself and not having to worry about other things.

Raleigh Team Manager Sam Wood helps rider Karen Murphy make vital last minute alterations to her bike before a race.

Competition licences are another thing I look after, because riders often forget them.''

Once the race is complete, Sam, in his capacity as Manager goes and collects all of the points and positions of the riders so that these can later be analysed and discover that if someone was in third position — why?

When major meetings can have up to 1,000 riders present from various factory teams, it can be seen why having a good manager is so essential. ''We even video some important meetings so that we can all get together and watch the race several times to look for where improvements can be made.''

This is usually done in the intensive training sessions that he puts them through. In the past, riders were often left to their own devices, but now it is becoming more like team work. ''The top riders are on a strict diet and training,'' he says. ''It's no use them stuffing themselves with junk food. They need to control their meals in just the same way that athletes do. You need to have tremendous power in your legs when you are racing and the proper approach to food is required prior to a meeting.

Even top riders like Andy Ruffell appreciate the advice and help given by Sam Wood.

"The training itself is often done at our training camp and the top riders are expected to do 40 miles per day on a 10 speed racer. They must also practise around 50 to 100 starts on a starting gate, because in competitions those first few yards are the most important in controlling the lead.

"After this, the boys can relax on BMX bikes for a while and practise their stunts. We don't make them do any training on a Saturday because the events take place on a Sunday and the riders need to be completely relaxed and rested before them."

So just how do new riders find their way into the team? "There are various ways, but I find that I'm inundated with letters or calls from prospective riders. I do read all the applications. But if someone has taken the effort to do a proper c.v. and list their recent results and so on then I take a greater interest. There are some riders who are very good at the local level and I try to see some of them performing, and if they are good then they'll get some form of sponsorship. The sport's still young enough for new riders to make it into a team!"

# WIN A RALEIGH BURNER!

Yes, you could win a fabulous RALEIGH BURNER. We are giving away 2 of these famous bikes in this easy to enter competition. All you have to do is design the ultimate BMX track, taking into consideration all skill and safety factors. The competition closing date is March 31, 1986 and the 2 winners will be notified by May 1, 1986. Entries should be sent to:

BMX RALEIGH BURNER COMPETITION,
Grandreams Ltd.,
Jadwin House,
205/211 Kentish Town Road,
London NW5 2JU.

All entrants should state their name, address and age. The publishers regret that designs cannot be returned. The editor's decision is final.

# CRAIG SCHOFIELD

## ~ seeing the world on a bike.

# CRAIG SCHOFIELD
## ~ seeing the world on a bike.

For Craig Schofield, being a member of a BMX team has meant that he has had the opportunity to travel the world. And he is relishing every moment of it. And in some cases the countries that he has visited in the course of racing and other associated work has been quite unusual.

"Probably the most interesting was a trip that I

# CRAIG SCHOFIELD

## ~ seeing the world on a bike.

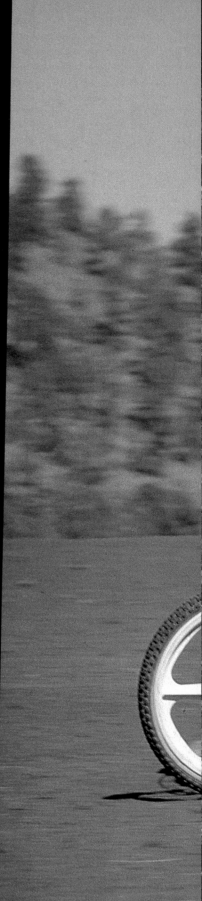

had to do to Israel,'' he says. ''The sport was only just starting there and I was sent out to do some promotional work on the bikes. This involved doing some exhibition and promotional appearances. You find that when you go to a country that hasn't been all that involved in the sport the interest it arouses is tremendous.

''Once I'd been there he sport really picked up and Israel is fast becoming a major BMX country now,'' he says. ''Italy was interesting too and there was a lot of excitement generated by the visits there.'' He says that they were particularly impressed with the trick riding and that the kids were anxious to try their own hand at some of the freestyle manoeuvres.

In addition to these countries, Craig has also travelled all round Europe, to Japan, Australia and America, three times each and is now looking for fresh fields to conquer!

''When I went to Japan, it was for the World Championships and I was wondering just what to expect. That's because you know that you are up against the best. What was probably disappointing was that the American riders didn't turn up for some reason or other, but most of the BMX nations were represented.

''In all, I guess there was something like 1,500 riders there, but these were all top class and things were tough. For instance, you have to qualify to be able to compete. This consisted of three races to be able to put you through into the eight, and then so on to the quarters and semis before the final.''

Craig, talented rider that he is, came fourth in the World which he says: ''Was a pleasant sensation.'' And he is now looking forward to more World Championship competitions in future years.

''I think what got to me most of all was the level

seem to be affected by the climate when I'm racing. And the track, considering it was for a World Championship could have been a lot better.''

Heat was a problem for Craig in Australia too. ''I've been out there on my own to practise,'' he says. ''I paid for my own trip during the winter, because I wanted new competition and hopefully a nice dry atmosphere. But it proved to be too hot and I had to return to England.''

Most of the major BMX racers in this country who are riding full time, like Craig, use the winter months to practise. There are quite a few meetings around the country,'' he says, ''but these tend to be of a more local nature. So we use the winter for a kind of build up for the season proper which usually runs from March to somewhere in October. This is when all of the proper and important events take place.

''I'll either stick to my strict training schedule which often involves weightlifting to provide the stamina I need in races, or else I'll fly to

America and try to get in some practise there where there are a good number of other riders to compete against."

Craig says that the important events on the calendar for him are the UKBMX and NBMX competitions, the European series, and World Championship. "Other things do present themselves, but it's finding the time.

"As a full time member of a team I'm naturally involved with a lot of other activities. For instance, I'm frequently called upon to open shops or visit tracks around the country. Some of these might be new ones and they like to do a small ceremony to officially declare them in use.

"There's also quite a bit of television work to do, and then people are always wanting photographs and sessions have to be fitted in. When you add to this the usual five hours of strenuous training I do, including quite a few miles on an ordinary bi

# CRAIG SCHOFIELD
## ~ seeing the world on a bike.

...then I don't really find much time for leisure activities."

Craig says that travelling as a member of a team is particularly exciting. "The thing is, that although we are essentially a team, we race as individuals. So when we are competing we are really doing what we can for ourselves. But at the same time we are trying to do well for the team. So you get your own personal points and those which are accumulated for the team.

"So far things have been working rather nicely for Andy Ruffell and myself, because we fall into different categories and we've managed to stay on a winning streak. I think that all being roughly around the same age helps too. Like when we all went to Spain for the competitions there, there were five busloads of us and we had a marvellous time.

"But when you've had a good day on the track there isn't any major team celebration as such. You are really celebrating your own success!"

That said, Craig still feels that the team spirit definitely prevails and that he and all the other members are always elated when they come out top of the tables!

As for the bike which he uses, he says that he sticks to the same one and doesn't swap and alter too much. "I think you get used to the machine once you reach a certain stage. But I do like my bike to be in a pristine condition. What tends to happen in the events is that the frame can get in a pretty bad state. So I have a couple of frames which are identical and every month I send one back to be completely resprayed and done up like new. It's a nice way of doing things and I always have a decent looking bike.

"Other than that I rarely make any changes other than replacement of worn components on the bike.

"Every member of a team is responsible for

# CRAIG SCHOFIELD

## ~ seeing the world on a bike.

looking after his own machine. But with the younger members, they'll be given expert help if and when they need it.''

Craig is doing all he can to promote the sport. ''I'm also interested in cars,'' he says, ''and I like messing around with them. But I don't think you can beat BMX for safety and excitement!''

*A*nyone who is contemplating going in for track racing as opposed to freestyle always has to come up against the varying types of track which are now made available to the sport. Not only this, but he or she also needs to be able to adapt to the impositions that the weather can create. Riders who turn up unprepared on just how they can improve their bike with fine, if simple changes to their machine, often lose out to those who took the time and trouble to learn a few tricks of the trade; obvious though they might be.

If, for instance, the weather is kind, then the best thing to use is a composition tyre, or what is better known as a heavily treaded tyre. But, if however, using the same track it should turn out to be wet and the surface was to become loose and bumpy, then the best thing a rider can do is to set the tyre pressures down a bit.

Should you not do this then you might find yourself encountering a lot of spin. It is also recommended that you drop the gearing a bit because this would mean that you wouldn't have to pedal so hard.

Racing on indoor tracks or concrete surfaces means that it is useful to be working with something like Michelin street tyres or similar; a smooth tyre with normal tread. In fact, an old trick which most riders use is to cover the tyre with a film of hair spray. It doesn't do the tyres any good, but it certainly helps them grip! So if you can afford to be a bit lavish on the tyres, it's something worth thinking about, if only occasionally.

A frequent misconception is that tracks on the North American circuit must be superior to those in Britain, if only based on the fact that the sport has been in existence longer there than anywhere else. In fact, the Americans do not have

necessarily better tracks than here; but they do have better weather! This means that there is, of course, a greater consistency for the riders. The West Coast of America is ideal because of its climate!

A recent innovation in track design has been worked in Birmingham for the Kellogg's Championships. In the first of these televised competitions, tracks were selected at different venues and held weekly. This meant that riders taking part had to travel extensively in order to compete.

# B.M.X. TRACKS
## -BE PREPARED!

*Left, centre and below:* 3 photographs that show vividly some of the aspects of BMX track racing.

What has been done now, is to develop a track whereby there are a couple of start hills in each corner of the track coming away from each other. This has been designed purely for the televising of the event, which is now going to be filmed all in one week. The impression that is created by using the multi start tracks is that different venues have been used. But it is certainly going to ease the strain on riders and their travelling time.

Birmingham certainly features strongly as a centre for BMX track favourites, but

Craig Schofield (right) successfully negotiates one of the many jumps that is common to most BMX tracks.

there are also many other good venues around the country. Notably these are at Slough, Bournemouth, Poole, Chertsey, Coxmoor, Sennleys, Illingham, Wigan, and Harwick Park.

Creating a BMX track of good standard requires expert advice, even when it is of a local type and there are certain rules which must be

stuck to if the people involved wish to provide the best for their riders.

The most important aspect for a good track is the starting gate which must have the ability to be controlled either manually or electronically and it should have a mandatory height of at least 18ins. with a starting line elevated to around 8ft.

naturally converge after the start, but there must be room to enable overtaking and, consequently, this width must be kept for the entire length of the track!

The obstacles themselves need particular care and attention and it is suggested that the first berm be not less than 75ft from the start and situated at an angle of not more than 145°. Any distance less than this and you run the possibility of the riders not having established themselves in position and too many riders converging on the berm at the same time. An angle greater than that suggested would also inhibit smooth progress.

It is also recommended that the jumps should be shaped and perfectly safe for the riders allowing a follow through before they reach the next of the obstacles to negotiate.

For the usual one lap races, a track of around 300 to 400 metres in length is necessary. Safety is of paramount importance around the perimeter of the track. Particular care should be made to remove any obstacles likely to be a danger to the riders, particularly in the event of a rider coming off.

These might be in the form of posts, wire and rocks. The track should also be constantly checked for anything which could impede rider flow. It is also advisable to place barriers of straw bales at strategic places where riders are likely to have crashes.

If all of these details are attended to then there is no reason why a good BMX track cannot be built and the expert advice can often be obtained from either of the major BMX associations!

The hill should also run for around 40ft and be around 24ft wide. A problem that is often encountered if these measurements are not adhered to is, that reduced width encourages more crashes at the commencement of a race which is not fair to riders, spoils the enjoyment of the spectators and frustrates the organizers of the events.

The course should be an open ended one and irregular since both right and left hand turns have to be negotiated. There should also be a suitable number of hills, jumps and whoops.

Whilst the width of the start is recommended to be at 24ft, the track itself can be from 15ft in width. Riders

# KAREN MURPHY

## talks about the problems facing girl riders.

# KAREN MURPHY

## ~talks about the problems facing girl riders.

Girl riders are still in a minority as regard the BMX sport, but the slowly increasing numbers now actively participating has managed to level out some of the inequalities of opportunity that had prevailed.

Karen Murphy is one such rider who has experienced the paucity of competition in earlier years

# KAREN MURPHY
## ~talks about the problems facing girl riders.

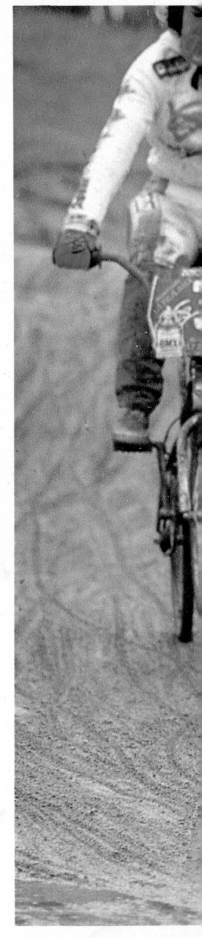

and is now enjoying a much higher standard of racing. Her original dissatisfaction is quite justified: "I'd find that when I turned up for a competition there would literally be only one gateful for the girls out of maybe 1,500 boys competing. This meant that the winner was chosen on a sole race.

"It was still fun and enjoyable, but it meant an awful lot of travelling for just that one race. Now, there are sufficient girls in the Nationals for us to be able to have several gatefuls, a semi-final and final which makes much more of a competition for us."

Hopefully, as more and more girls are attracted to the sport, the level of competition is going to increase. Fifteen year old Karen says: "You notice how good the girls in France are, particularly. I went over there to compete and I was impressed by the standards they've achieved."

Karen began racing a couple of years ago after acquiring her first BMX bike.

"I suppose, like a lot of girls, I wasn't fully aware of the amount of competitions that existed until some friends of mine told me about these special events. So I found one that was close to my home town and went along and learnt all about the pointing system.

"At my first attempt I managed an overall rating of ninth place, and by the second year I was graded at 2nd. That fortunately led to me obtaining my first sponsorship. There are scouts from many of the major companies at the

Nationals and so I was approached. I later switched to Raleigh and have been with them ever since.''

It has now led to opportunities to travel around the world which she squeezes in at weekends. But she is sensible enough to realise that her schoolwork is also important. ''I wouldn't want to bank everything on being able to become a professional rider,'' she says.

Even so, she practises every night and is forever trying to do jumps from different approach angles. ''As far as I'm concerned, this is one of the most important elements in my training. In racing you cannot hope for the perfect approach to a jump. The whole thing is determined by the required speed and what other riders are doing around

# KAREN MURPHY

-talks about
the problems facing
girl riders.

you. So I like to be able to practise for any eventuality arising from a race.''

Karen also likes to do try outs on lots of different surfaces in varying weather conditions. ''I like to be prepared,'' she says. ''I really think that the worst possible surface for competing on is sand or a wet surface. I try to adjust my gearing for this, but there can be an awful lot of slipping and sliding.

''I also try not to stay in the air for too long when I'm racing because that's time lost. So it needs to be a good clean jump with the minimum of aerial contact.

''The other area that takes a lot of time in my practise is that of the starting gate. No matter how good you are on the track, everything hinges on a good start. Your race can be won

# KAREN MURPHY
## ~talks about the problems facing girl riders.

or lost according to how good a gate you manage. So I don't think you can concentrate enough on this. Even if you are brilliant, it's something you must keep on practising in case you become complacent about it!''

As to her own bike, Karen says that like most riders, she is constantly trying to improve her machine. ''There are just so many new products coming onto the market all the time. I'm fortunate in that I'm sponsored as part of a team and I have a good team manager. This means that if I do feel that I can improve my riding because of fitting a new component that suits my bike's specification then all I have to do is to ask the team manager, and he can supply it for me. But there is no pressure on myself or any of

the other riders to experiment with new components. It's left entirely up to us to find what we feel most comfortable with and which provides the best performance in competition!

Much as she enjoys racing, she does think that things could be made easier for many riders.

''I don't think that the overall BMX sport can be improved, because it's pretty well organized already. But what I think would help immensely is if many of the National events could be divided originally into something like North and South. From these competitions, a whole batch of winners in varying age categories could be found.

''The finals would then be held at a specific venue for the top Southern and Northern riders to compete. I

# KAREN MURPHY

## ~talks about the problems facing girl riders.

don't think it would complicate things too much and it would certainly ease the tremendous burden of travelling that most of us have to do.''

Perhaps this is something the associations might well consider and it certainly makes sense when some competitions don't finish until nine in the evening!

# BIKE MAINTENANCE
## -MAKE OR BREAK

It doesn't really matter whether you are a top class racing competitor, a stunt enthusiast, a local level rider, or just a plain fan of a BMX which you want to ride in your nearest park; the major thing that you cannot ignore is bike maintenance.

As a good rider can tell you, not only is it essential for the safety of yourself, but it is going to make your machine perform much better and last longer if you ignore the obvious.

Here then is a check list which you should follow whether you are preparing for a competetive event, or if you are just going for a relaxing ride. And remember, that all of these things should be checked regularly after rides, too, since not only are the stunts liable to cause some problems, but the mud and the grit that you attract aren't kind to any type of machine.

## Brakes:

The first thing that you should look for, is that there are absolutely no frayed cables. They should always be kept nice and tidy. The brakes themselves should always be adjusted properly. So often they are not and it is incredible how many riders do not pay the care and attention they should to worn brake blocks. If they need replacing then do so as soon as possible. It is a danger to yourself and others to neglect this important part of the bike. They should be adjusted so that they sit on the rim properly. And just because you have done the job a couple of times doesn't mean it'll last. Make certain you repeatedly check them.

## Handlebar Grips:

It is essential that you look to make sure that there is no dangerous metal sticking out so that you don't puncture anyone else. Where close riding conditions are involved this is a potential hazard.

## Handlebar Stem:

This should always be tight, because if it isn't then you are going to have steering problems and that can lead to accidents. Always check this before every ride because it is the most common thing to work loose.

It is advisable to use a four bolt system and not the two bolt as is sometimes found in design. The four bolt system is much stronger and safer.

## Seat Post and Saddle:

This should always be tight and secure and not be able to move in any way. You can avoid a lot of problems with careful attention to this. Also you should replace any worn bits as soon as possible.

## The Frame:

You should always be on the look out for cracks, no matter how fine, or for broken welds. The kind of action that a BMX is expected to withstand is heavy, and no matter how stringent factory tests are, normal wear and tear can produce such cracks, especially if the bike is not used properly or is used for a lot of heavy duty racing. Also check for bent forks or drop outs and that they are serviceable and not worn.

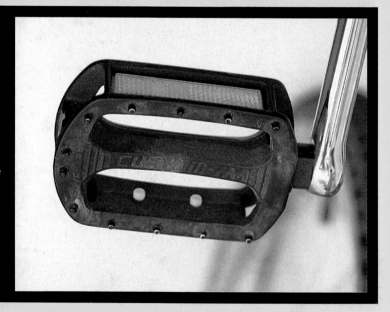

## Bearings:

It is the head set bearing which is the most common to work loose, but it is important to note that when you are tightening it, you should not overtighten it. Just sufficiently so that it does not move.

The bottom bracket bearing mustn't be swinging loose either, but it should spin freely without any excessive play.

## Pedals:

The pedals on BMX bikes, as you are aware, are specially designed so that the feet won't slip on them. These are usually of the studded or jaw type. In either case, any form of wear should require immediate replacement or sharpening to ensure firm footing.